*T*o all mothers who will be completing this book....

In filling in this book for your daughter you will create
perhaps the most valuable gift you could ever give.
I hope you will create a book for your daughter to treasure,
full of your life's memories. Each item you write down
will be recorded here for your daughter
to read over and over again – and for her to pass down
to her family. Because each thought is written down
it becomes a keepsake for life.

I encourage you to change the book to fit your life
– some of you may have been divorced,
or may have been adopted as a child.
Glue totally unsuitable pages together!
Indeed, glue in special memorabilia and cross out
headings that don't work for you.
You can even glue a photograph of yourself
over this introduction.
The more messed up, crossed out and personal
your final gift is, the more precious, the more genuine
it will be.

Helen Exley

To my daughter

With love from

IN THE SAME SIZE AND FORMAT AS THIS BOOK:

Grandmother Remembers
A Sister Remembers
A Family Record Book
Baby Record Book

OTHER HELEN EXLEY GIFTBOOKS:

My Daughter, My Joy
To a very special **Daughter**
To a very special **Mother**
To a lovely Mother
A gem of a Daughter

Published in 2011 by Helen Exley Giftbooks in Great Britain.

EDITED BY HELEN EXLEY

2 4 6 8 10 12 11 9 7 5 3 1

Illustrations by Juliette Clarke.
Selection and arrangement copyright © Helen Exley 2011.
Illustrations © Helen Exley 2011.
The moral right of the author has been asserted.

ISBN: 978-1-84634-487-9

Printed in China.

Helen Exley Giftbooks, 16 Chalk Hill, Watford, Herts WD19 4BG, UK
www.helenexleygiftbooks.com

A Mother Remembers

Written with love for my daughter

ILLUSTRATED BY JULIETTE CLARKE

A HELEN EXLEY GIFTBOOK

Contents

GREAT GRANDMOTHER

GREAT GRANDFATHER

GREAT GRANDMOTHER

GREAT GRANDFATHER

GRANDMOTHER

GRANDFATHER

YOUR FAMILY TREE

There has never been anyone quite like you.
You took a little from everyone who came before you.
You are woven from a thousand lives – the family
that came before you. Each has given you a gift –
each has played a part in what you are.

GREAT GRANDMOTHER

GREAT GRANDFATHER

GREAT GRANDMOTHER

GREAT GRANDFATHER

GRANDMOTHER

GRANDFATHER

MOTHER

FATHER

NAME

The history of my family

The earliest history and origin of the family

Great historical events – wars, peace, natural disasters that affected our family

Social changes that affected us

Financial background and changes in our family

Important family events

Medical histories, important causes of death

Occupations

Talents and achievements

Other stories and memories

My grandparents

My grandparents' details

_____

_____

When and how they lived

_____

_____

How my grandfather earned his living

_____

Their talents

_____

_____

_____

My grandparents' details

_____

_____

When and how they lived

_____

_____

How my grandfather earned his living

_____

_____

_____

Their talents

Health history and important information

Things I've been told

My grandmothers' lives

Things I've been told about their lives and families

_____

_____

_____

How women dressed

_____

What they did for fun

_____

How they would have spent their lives

_____

About their talents and their loves

_____

What rights did women have then?

_____

What household tasks did a woman have?

_____

New inventions and changes in their lifetime

_____

_____

More information

_____

_____

_____

Children are uncertain about time.
Did Grandma grow up without
electricity, or was that Great Grandmother?
Who was alive when man first
walked on the moon?
My grandmother saw her world
turned upside down.
As my mother and then I did.
As you will.
It's part of the adventure.

My mother

Her maiden name

_____

Why her first names were chosen

_____

Her birth date, birthplace and important facts

_____

_____

_____

Her education

_____

_____

_____

Family life

_____

_____

_____

Her greatest adventures

_____

_____

_____

Her talents and skills

_____

_____

_____

Stories she told

_____

_____

_____

_____

Her hopes, dreams and plans

_____

_____

Why is it so important
to include my mother in a book
dedicated to you?
Because she is a part
of you and me.

The things she liked and disliked most

The things she feared most

Her hardest times

Her funniest memories

Her happiest times

Her greatest achievement/s

Other important facts and events

Mother's house was a treasure trove
of memories; mementos filled every space
and covered every wall.
The wonderful smell of fresh home baking
filled the air and the atmosphere
exuded love and peace.
Any worry, pain or sadness was quickly
soothed away.

When my mother was young

Memories she shared with us

The great world events when she was a child

Great world events when she grew up

The medical advances and how they affected her life and world

The great inventions in her life

Books/great people who changed her life

The political changes in her lifetime

Memories of my mother

Important memories of my mother

_____

_____

_____

What she was like to me when I was younger

_____

_____

My mother's personality

_____

Her greatest strengths

_____

Her personal values

_____

Sad things in her life

_____

The sacrifices she made

_____

_____

What has made my mother so special to me

_____

_____

_____

_____

My father

His name, birth date, birthplace and important facts

_____

_____

His education

_____

Family life

_____

_____

_____

His greatest achievements

_____

_____

His talents and skills

_____

_____

His hobbies and interests

_____

_____

His hopes, dreams, plans

_____

_____

_____

_____

Things he liked and disliked most

Things he feared most

His hardest times

His funniest stories/memories

His happiest times

His greatest disappointments

Other important and interesting things

That quiet mutual gaze
of a trusting husband and wife is like
the first moment of rest or refuge
from a great weariness or great danger.

GEORGE ELIOT [MARY ANN EVANS] (1819-1880)

My parents' wedding

Date _____ Place _____

My parents' wedding day
_____

_____

How my parents met
_____

_____

What attracted my mother to my father
_____

_____

Stories they have told of their romance and courtship
_____

_____

_____

The proposal
_____

_____

What my mother told me about her wedding day
_____

_____

Their honeymoon
_____

_____

There is nothing nobler or more
admirable than when two people
who see eye to eye
keep house as man and wife,
confounding their enemies
and delighting their friends.

HOMER (c.700 B.C.)

Marriage and home

Where my parents lived
_____

What their home/s looked like
_____

_____

Their financial state
_____

_____

Their struggles
_____

_____

Their successes
_____

_____

What occupation/s they had
_____

_____

What they liked about each other
_____

_____

How world events affected their lives
_____

_____

_____

_____

Stories I have heard about their life together
_____

_____

_____

Stories about the family – and special memories
_____

_____

_____

Me!

The names I was given when I was born

_____

The reason for those names

_____

_____

My pet names, my nicknames

_____

Important facts

_____

_____

_____

Memories of when I was very young

_____

_____

_____

What I disliked and feared

_____

_____

_____

Stories about me as a baby

_____

_____

_____

_____

The best of my memories

Summer days.
Making cakes.
Building sandcastles.
Dad swinging me to the sky.
A gentle puppy,
butterflies and a robin.
Stories, games.
Hide and Seek.
Little things to remember
for a lifetime.

CHARLOTTE GRAY

Childhood days

My earliest memories

Stories about me when I was little

My talents and achievements

Early fears

Memories of my home

Memories of my family

Memories of friends

My best memories of my childhood

Growing years

Early adventures

_____

_____

_____

Sad times

_____

_____

Happy times

_____

_____

_____

_____

Things that formed my character

_____

_____

_____

My first loves – animals, pop stars, sports

_____

_____

_____

Things I disliked most

_____

_____

_____

Memories of school-days

Things I'll never forget

...as I grew I acquired things – more and more things
– the debris from every enthusiasm I'd adopted.
Glue and balsa wood and model planes,
ballet shoes and rock suspected of holding fossils,
sea shells, worn toys – among them a dozen
Teddy Bears. It was my room, my territory.
A summing up of all that was me.

PAM BROWN, B.1928

My room, my life as a child

What my room was like

Fashions when I was a child

Preposterous clothes I wore as a child

The things I loved

My hobbies and interests

Memories of school

Thoughts when I was quiet

Other thoughts I'd like to share with you

The teenage years

Happy and sad memories of my teenage years

Things about the world that made me sad

Fashions when I was a teenager

My first dance, my first kiss

Preposterous clothes I wore

My early strong values and beliefs

My first passions and major interests

_____

_____

_____

_____

Other special firsts

_____

_____

_____

_____

_____

_____

_____

_____

_____

_____

Daydreaming

What I dreamed about

_____

_____

_____

My concerns – deep thoughts

_____

_____

What I wanted to be

_____

_____

My hopes for the world and what I believed in

_____

_____

Anxiety and excitements about growing up

_____

_____

Broken dreams

_____

_____

Dreams that have stayed with me

_____

_____

_____

I loved to dream,
to have time to do absolutely nothing.
To sit in a field or hide
or to retire to my room to dream and scheme.
Time enough for riding the bike
and wading through fallen leaves.
But I needed to draw breath.
To have space. To think of my future,
of my hopes.

We talked together of books
that have been important.
We shared the overwhelming delight in
a picture, a play, a poem, a piece of music.
We cheered for the same team.
We loved walking the high hills.
These things are what made me what I am.
All we have loved has made it possible
to see with each other's eyes.

Together – my mother and me

Our happiest times

Sad times

Things we did together

The things we had in common

Things that made us laugh

Shared times

What she taught me

The kindest things she did

Special memories of sharing

For all of us,
for three generations of women,
the world has changed
– profoundly.

Being a woman

I listened to the stories my mother told me – of how she had to
leave school early to go out and work – yet her brother stayed on.
How little freedom she had. The world has changed
completely for me. And yet for all women, it's just beginning.

My mother's best story about growing up – as a woman

The barriers most women faced

The obstacles she faced

The dreams she had for her life

Her greatest "victories"

Her greatest successes and failures

How things have changed for women as I grew up

What obstacles remained for me

My successes and failures

Love and romance

How I met Dad

...about falling in love

What I most liked about him

What he most liked about me

Romantic moments

WHATEVER OUR SOULS ARE MADE OF, HIS AND MINE ARE THE SAME.

EMILY BRONTË (1818-1848)

Our song, our special places

Obstacles we overcame

My special memories

Our hopes and dreams

Marriage is the fusion
of two hearts
– the union of two lives
– the coming together
of two tributaries.

PETER MARSHALL

My wedding

The date of our wedding

Your father's full name

About him – his life, his work, his family

What the wedding was like

My dress, the reception, all the details

Things that went wrong!

A description of my special, my lovely day

My happiest memories

Anything, everything,
little or big
becomes an adventure
when the right person shares it.

KATHLEEN NORRIS (1880-1966)

Our first years together

What we loved about each other

Things we did together

Our first home

Practical early problems

How we overcame problems

Things that made us laugh

Things we bought that I still treasure

Sad memories

The wonderful memories

You!

When and where you were born

What/who you looked like

My memories of that first day

Why we chose your name

How your birth changed my life

Things I learned the hard way

The world you were born into – world events and changes

My fears and hopes for your safety and your life

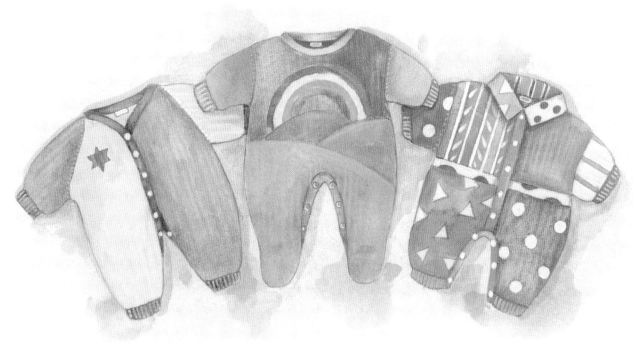

My hopes for you when you were born

Other special memories and thoughts

Every year I've lived has become
doubly valuable
since you came into this world.

One moment you were crawling on hands and knees,
the next you were so grown up.
I am blessed to have shared time with you.

STUART AND LINDA MACFARLANE

When you were young

What I thought of you

Things that made me laugh

What made me proud

Funny things you did or said

First school-days

Things you loved

What frightened you and calmed you

My happiest memories of you

You and me

The connection I have felt

What I've learned from you

What we have in common

Ways in which we are utterly different

Things that have hurt both of us

What has made me laugh/be happy

Sorrows we've shared

_____

_____

_____

Things we've enjoyed doing together

_____

_____

_____

_____

Mother and child, yes,
but sisters really,
    against whatever denies us
all that we are.

ALICE WALKER, B.1944

There have been times of trouble and anxiety
sorrow, depression, pain.
But they have been balanced out with good times.
Weekends when the sun shone.
Surprises. Astonishments. Achievements.
Times to remember.

Things I have loved

Books and authors

Movies/shows

Music, songs

Pets and animals

Food

Flowers, trees, nature

Places, countries

Hobbies, sports and activities

Things I'd like to share with you

I wish you so much,
but most of all I wish you courage.
Not battle-bravery, but the quiet courage
that endures, survives and never loses hope.
The courage that will sustain
you through every darkness,
the courage that will give strength to others.
The courage that will turn
what seems defeat into victory.

My beliefs, my passions

Important beliefs that have inspired my life

The great teachers

The great political leaders

"Ordinary", very extraordinary people in my life

Books that have changed my life

Great films, great artists

Historical changes and events that have affected/changed me

Central events in my own life that have changed me

I have such hopes for you –
not fame or riches,
though they may come,
but the enthusiasm to make bold choices,
to learn and experiment and make and do.
To weather storms.
To learn from failure.
To discover goodness in other people.

My hopes for you

I wish you the joy of this music I have loved

I wish you these extraordinary sights

...these books, these movies

...these special places

...moments of this kind of special love

Adventures I wish you

Things I wish I'd learned

Things I've never done, risks I've never taken that I hope you'll have the courage to

Other loves I wish you

My last important things

Take with you into your future all my love.
All the things we've seen together, all the music
we have heard, all the people we have met and loved,
all the secrets, all the giggling, all the mischiefs
we have made. I'll come with you as far as I'm allowed
along your road – and when we part you'll take with you
my hopes and half my heart.

Other important extras

For your choice of press cuttings, personal thoughts,
a loved poem, a special picture....

A letter from me to you